Practice Tests for Math GOAL 2 Level B, Forms 923M and 924M

Helping Learners Develop Mathematical Thinking Skills, Approach Math with Confidence, and Sharpen their Test-Taking Ability

By

TABLE OF CONTENTS

Dear Instructors,

This book entails four (4) practice tests and is designed to prepare adult learners for the CASAS Math GOALS 2, Level B Forms 923M and 924M. The practice tests align with the CASAS Competencies and meet the rigorous requirements of the College and Career Readiness Standards (CCRS), the National Reporting System (NRS), and the Workforce Innovation and Opportunity Act (WIOA).

Adhering to the CASAS Math GOALS 2 test blueprint, the practice tests assess learners' understanding of the following math areas: *Number Sense and Operations, Consumer Economics, Algebraic Thinking, Geometry, Data Analysis and Statistics, and Pure Mathematics.*

More importantly, this resource increases learners' confidence, guides them to reflect on their learning and progress, and helps them transfer their knowledge to other contexts. Each practice test includes real-world activities that promote deep understanding and practical application of mathematical concepts. An answer key also accompanies each test.

By using this resource, you can save time, distribute practice sessions over several weeks, and assess and reinforce your learners' understanding of math functions and concepts. To order class sets, visit cbledu.com.

The CBL Team,

Your Partner in Student Learning

Dear Math Students,

This resource will help you develop and reinforce your math skills and test-taking ability. It will prepare you for the CASAS Math GOALS 2 Level B test. The practice tests will assess your understanding of the following math areas: *Number Sense and Operations, Consumer Economics, Algebraic Thinking, Geometry, Data Analysis and Statistics, and Pure Mathematics.*

Important Strategies:

Follow the strategies below to develop and reinforce your mathematical thinking skills and test-taking ability.

1. Study and master the four operations (addition, subtraction, multiplication, and division). Learn several strategies to compute and perform operations.

2. Study and master the multiplication table by reviewing it at least once daily (5 to 10 minutes).

3. Look up the meanings of math concepts (e.g., *sum, product, quotient, fraction, triangle*). Try to describe their meanings in your own words.

4. Seek to understand math ideas or the big picture before practicing the details or simple exercises. You can do that by using YouTube videos or Khan Academy.

5. Connect math ideas and concepts to real-world objects or situations. Ask your instructors for real-life examples.

6. Ask clarifying questions to ensure you understand everything before your class ends.

7. Practice solving word problems weekly (20-30 minutes) without distraction (TV, PC, cellphone, noise).

8. Solve math operations and problems on paper. Always show your work—including your strategies or reasoning—on paper.

9. Study and practice math in a group or with a classmate. Discuss your math solutions and strategies.

10. Explain math ideas and concepts to yourself or someone else orally. After doing this orally, you can also do it using drawings and writing.

11. Always reflect on your progress and strategies. After each practice session or test, identify what works well and why you make certain mistakes. Review and focus on practicing math ideas and concepts you don't understand well.

12. Celebrate your achievements. Any increase in math knowledge is an achievement.

Remember, math skills are essential for success in various aspects of your life, including community involvement, managing family finances, and professional advancement. By committing to completing the practice tests in this book, you'll be setting yourself up for success in your academic pursuits and beyond.

Let's get to work!

Here are nine (9) practical ways you can overcome math fear and anxiety and build confidence while using this math book:

1. **Start Small:** Begin with easier problems that you can solve to build your confidence before solving harder ones.

2. **Use the book's Strategies:** Take advantage of this resource's strategies and practice tests. They are designed to help you understand, practice, and sharpen your math skills.

3. **Set Small Goals:** Break your math studies into small, achievable goals. Celebrate when you reach these goals to motivate yourself.

4. **Practice Regularly:** Consistent practice makes learning math more manageable. Try to work on math problems a few times a week.

5. **Take Breaks:** If you feel overwhelmed, take a short break. Come back to the math problems with a clear mind.

6. **Ask for Help:** Don't hesitate to seek help when you need it. Ask a teacher or a classmate, or use online resources if you're stuck.

7. **Stay Positive:** Keep a positive attitude about math. Remind yourself that you can handle it and that it's okay to make mistakes as you learn.

8. **Understand, Don't Memorize:** Focus on understanding the math ideas and concepts rather than just memorizing formulas. This understanding will make you feel more confident in solving math problems and taking math tests.

9. **Visualize Success:** Picture yourself successfully solving problems and understanding concepts. This visualization can boost your confidence.

By following these strategies, you will be able to study well and practice math with more confidence.

You have 60 minutes to answer 36 questions.

1. Which is another way to show 65, 671?

   A. 60,000 + 5,000 + 600 + 70 + 1

   B. 60,000 + 6,000 +500 + 70 + 1

   C. 6,000 + 5,000 + 600 + 70 + 1

   D. 600,000 + 5,000 + 600 + 70 + 1

2. In the number 863, 094, what digit is in the ten thousand place?

   A. 3

   B. 8

   C. 6

   D. 0

3. What is the value of the underlined digit?

$$\underline{3}, 987, 342$$

   A. Three hundred thousand

   B. Three hundred

   C. Three thousand

   D. Three million

4. The population of Hawaii is about 1, 142, 480 people. What is the correct way to write this number?

   A. One hundred forty-two thousand four hundred eighty

   B. One million one hundred forty-two thousand four hundred eighty

   C. One million one thousand forty-two thousand four hundred eighty

   D. One million one hundred fourteen-two thousand four hundred eighty

5. At a restaurant, the budget for utilities for an entire year is $24, 180. What would the monthly budget for utilities be?

   A. $1,980

   B. $2,100

   C. $2,150

   D. $2,015

6. If a server makes $21.85 per hour, including tips, how much would he make after working a 48-hour week?

   A. $1,080.40

   B. $1,048.80

   C. $1,200.15

   D. $1,049.75

7. Which of the following is a unit rate?

   A. 8 gallons/ 5 minutes

   B. 16 feet per second

   C. 0.45 miles

   D. $42.25

Look at the following table:

Item	Cost	Amount
A	$260	20 pounds
B	$352	32 pounds
C	$336	28 pounds
D	$450	30 pounds

8. What is the unit price of Item A in dollars per pound?

   A. $15 per pound

   B. $13 per pound

   C. $10 per pound

   D. $12 per pound

9. What is the unit price of Item C in dollar per pound?

   A. $12 per pound

   B. $9 per pound

   C. $14 per pound

   D. $15 per pound

10. What is the cost of 18 pounds of Item B?

   A. $200

   B. $198

   C. $216

   D. $220

11. What is the best deal?

   A. Item C

   B. Item D

   C. Item A

   D. Item B

Look at the following receipt:

Hotel Restaurant and Bar
1016 6th Ave
New York, NY
Tel: 650-309-1992

09/25/2020   12:54 PM
TERMINAL 2

1	Hendrick Gin & Tonic	$10.50
1	Ginger Mule	$9.50
1	Glass Camus Zin	$24.00
1	Titos Vodka Soda	?

Amount	**$60.76**
SUB-TOTAL	$56.00
TAX	?
BALANCE	$60.76
CREDIT CARD AUTH	VISA ####3993

12. How many items were purchased?

    A. 3   C. 5

    B. 6   D. 4

13. What is the tax amount?

    A. $5.76   C. $4.76

    B. $8.60   D. $4.90

14. What is the total amount?

    A. $56.00   C. $24.00

    B. $60.76   D. $58.76

15. What is the cost of a Titos Vodka Soda?

    A. $12.00   C. $11.50

    B. $13.50   D. $12.50

16. Which item is the cheapest?

    A. Titos Vodka Soda   C. Ginger Mule

    B. Hendrick Ging Tonic   D. Glass Camus Zin

17. What is the cost of six Ginger Mules?

    A. $56.50   C. $58.00

    B. $57.00   D. $59.50

18. Which of the following is equal to $17 (10 - 5)$?

    A. $27 - 85$ C. $170 + 85$

    B. $10 (17 - 5)$ D. $170 - 85$

19. What is the missing number?

$$59 \times 113 = 113 \times \,?$$

    A. 59   C. 54

    B. 113   D. 213

20. Six friends share the cost of a trip. The bill is $1,536. How much does each person pay?

    A. $276   C. $256

    B. $245   D. $250

21. Solve the following equation:

$$10x - 10 = 100$$

    A. $x = 10$ C. $x = 15$

    B. $x = 20$ D. $x = 11$

22. On a test, the highest grade is 16 points higher than the lowest grade. The sum of the two grades is 166. What is the lowest grade?

    A. 75   C. 68

    B. 78   D. 91

23. Four times a number is equal to 484. What is the equation that represents this situation?

    A. $4x = 484$ C. $x + 484 = 4$

    B. $x + 4 = 484$ D. $484x = 4$

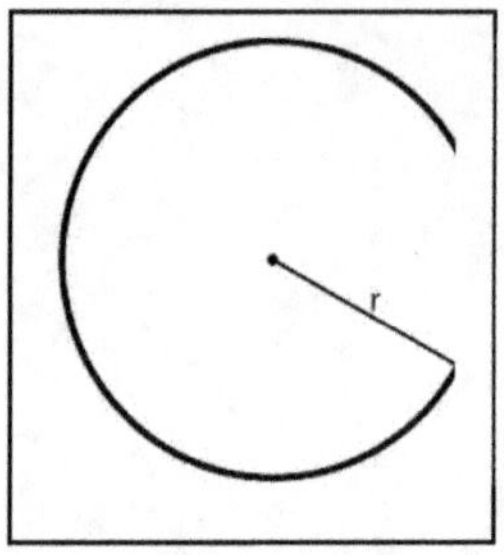

The formula for the circumference of the circle is

$$C = 2\pi r$$

C is the circumference of the circle and r is its radius.

24. What is the circumference of the circle if the radius is 2.5 feet? (Use $\pi = 3.14$)

A. 7.85 ft.
C. 14.13 ft.
B. 23.55 ft.
D. 15.7 ft.

25. If the circumference of the circle is 31.4 inches, what is the radius? (Use $\pi = 3.14$)

A. 10 in.
C. 15 in.
B. 5 in.
D. 20 in.

26. If the circumference of the circle is 56.52 inches, what is the area? (Use $\pi = 3.14$)

A. 127.17 in^2
C. 254.34 in^2
B. 200.96 in^2
D. 150.72 in^2

The perimeter of the following rectangle is 76.

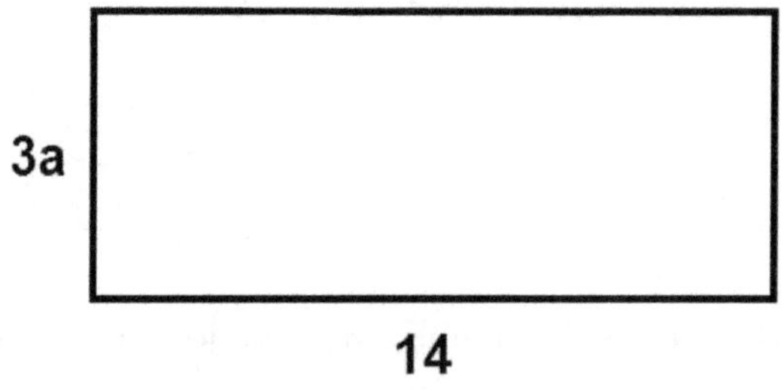

27. What is a?

A. 10
C. 6
B. 8
D. 12

28. What is the area of the rectangle?

A. 420
C. 336
B. 126
D. 168

29. Which of the following is a metric unit of length?

A. Feet span

B. Barrel

C. Feet

D. Millimeter

30. Mr. Foster is measuring out a small quantity of powder to put in a capsule. What units will he use to measure the mass of the powder?

A. Ton

B. Pound

C. Kilogram

D. Milligram

31. Which of the following is true?

A. A centimeter is smaller than a meter.

B. A paper clip is a metric unit of length.

C. A fluid ounce is a metric unit of volume.

D. A gallon is a non-standard unit of volume.

32. How many gallons are in 480 quarts?

A. 240 gal.

B. 120 gal.

C. 150 gal.

D. 125 gal.

33. Anthony purchased 12.50 meters of electrical wire, and Chloe purchased 7,500 centimeters of electrical wire. What is the total length in meters of wire that both of them purchased?

A. 19.50 m.

B. 1,250 m

C. 87.5 m.

D. 21.50 m.

Bruce recorded how much time he spent reading over five days. The following table shows the results.

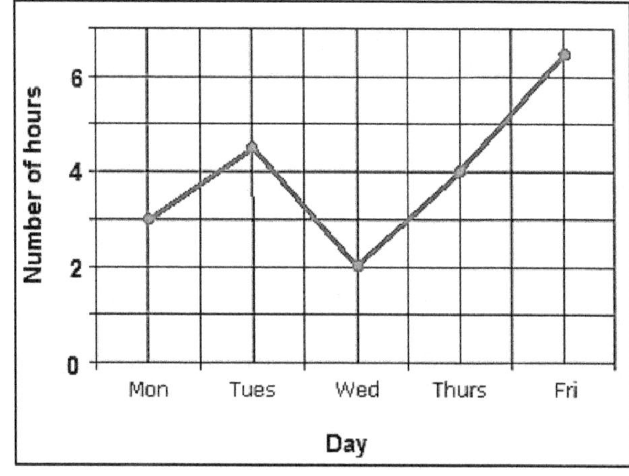

34. How many hours did he spend reading on Wednesday?

    A. 2 hours   C. 3 hours

    B. 5 hours   D. 6 hours

35. About how many hours did he spend reading on Tuesday?

    A. 4 hours   C. 5 hours

    B. 4.8 hours   D. 4.5 hours

36. On which day did he read for four hours?

    A. Friday   C. Monday

    B. Thursday   D. Tuesday

Answer Key:

1. A	19. A
2. C	20. C
3. D	21. D
4. B	22. A
5. D	23. A
6. B	24. D
7. B	25. B
8. B	26. C
9. A	27. B
10. B	28. C
11. D	29. D
12. D	30. D
13. C	31. A
14. B	32. B
15. A	33. C
16. C	34. A
17. B	35. D
18. D	36. B

REFLECTION ON LEARNING

After completing Practice Test #1, reflect on your performance by answering the questions below. Discuss your responses with your instructor or a classmate.

1. What questions did you answer incorrectly? List the question numbers.

2. Review the list. What types of questions (operations, measurements, algebra, geometry, data analysis, statistics, graph, pie chart) did you answer incorrectly?

3. Review each question you've missed. Why do you think you answered the question incorrectly?

4. Based on the questions you missed, what math functions or concepts do you need to study and practice more? List them.

5. Review the question you got correctly. What strategies or methods did you use? What did you do well?

6. After reviewing all the questions, what questions do you have for your instructor?

You have 60 minutes to answer 36 questions.

1. In the number 76,143, what digit is in the thousand place?

   A. 1   C. 6

   B. 7   D. 4

2. Kevin drives 18.75 miles from City A to City B. What is this number in word form?

   A. Eighty and seventy-five hundredths   C. Eighty and seventy-five thousandths

   B. Eighteen and seventy-five   D. Eighteen and seventy-five hundredths
   thousandths

3. Lucas has $898.90 in his checking account. How much does he have in his account after he makes a deposit of $346.73 and a withdrawal of $298.98?

   A. $946.65   C. $253.19

   B. $1, 245.63   D. $846.75

4. Cindy studied a total of 41.3 hours over a period of five days. On average, how many hours did Cindy study each day?

   A. 6.1 hours   C. 5.5 hours

   B. 8.26 hours   D. 7.4 hours

5. Compute

$$\frac{1}{3}\left(\frac{3}{4} - \frac{1}{6}\right)$$

   A. $\dfrac{5}{12}$ C. $\dfrac{7}{36}$

   B. $\dfrac{7}{12}$ D. $\dfrac{2}{3}$

6. Mark can mow a lawn that measures 1, 350 square feet in 2.5 hours. At that rate, how long would it take him to mow a lawn of 6,750 square feet?

   A. 10 hours   B. 9.5 hours

C. 8 hours   D. 12.5 hours

Look at the following table:

Item	Cost
Book	$19.75
Speakers	$66.99
Bedsheet	$18.55
Charging cable	$7.99

7. What is the total cost of two books and four speakers?

A. $240.47   C. $345.67

B. $307.46   D. $308.99

8. If Luke spent $111.30 on bedsheets, how many did he buy?

A. 7   C. 9

B. 6   D. 4

9. Which item is the cheapest?

A. Speakers   C. Charging cable

B. Book   D. Bedsheet

Look at the following receipt:

```
            EYE OF THAI-GER
           3077 Stone Lane
           Philadelphia, PA

    9/12/2018        11:54 AM
    TAB49
    AMEX        HOST ALIA
    QTY      DESC              AMT
    - - - - - - - - - - - - - - - - - - - - - - -
    1        31. Part Ka Pow      $8.99
    1        Steam Rice           $4.00
    1        Red Curry            $8.99
    1        add Beef             $0.00
    1        19. Pad Thai         $8.99
    2        Thai Ice Tea w/boba  $13.00
    1        water                $0.00


    AMT             $43.97

    SUB - TOTAL     $43.97
    TAX             $3.34
    BALANCE         ?
```

10. How many items were purchased?

   A. 8   C. 9

   B. 7   D. 6

11. What is the sub-total amount?

   A. $3.34   C. $46.77

   B. $43.97   D. $43.28

12. What is the total amount?

   A. $43.97   C. $46.97

   B. $44.55   D. $47.31

13. How much would six iced tea cost?

   A. $6.50   C. $39

   B. $13   D. $45.50

14. What is the cost of five Pad Thai?

   A. $44.95   C. $45.16

   B. $44.76   D. $43.85

15. What is the value of Z?

$$16 \times 83 \times 72 = 83 \times 72 \times Z$$

A. 83

C. 72

B. 16

D. 83 x 72

16. Which expression is equivalent to 52 x 705?

A. 705 x 50 x 2

C. 52 x 700 x 5

B. 52 (70 + 5)

D. 52 (700 + 5)

17. Solve the following equation:

$$15 + 7x = 64$$

A. 7

C. 6

B. 8

D. 12

18. Fast 2200 rents bikes for $16 plus $4 per hour. Scott paid $38 to rent a bike. For how many hours did he rent the bike?

A. 6 hours

C. 8 hours

B. 6.5 hours

D. 5.5 hours

Look at the following triangle:

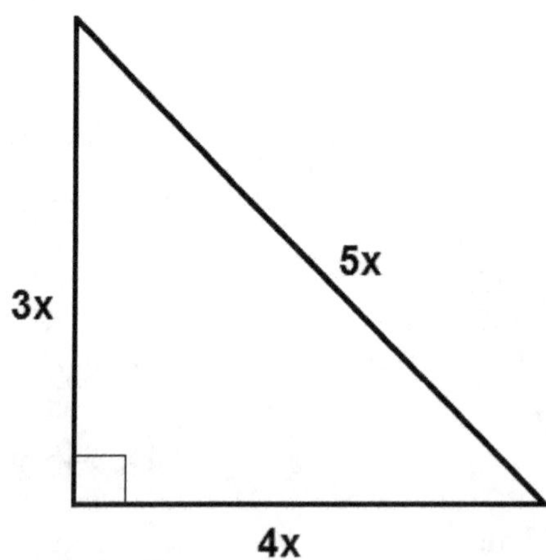

19. If the perimeter of the triangle is 120 inches, what is x?

A. 12

C. 15

B. 10

D. 9

20. What is the area of the triangle?

A. 450 in^2 C. 100 in^2

B. 500 in^2 D. 600 in^2

21. Suppose that x = 6 inches, what is the perimeter of the triangle?

A. 54 inches   C. 72 inches

B. 68 inches   D. 75 inches

The perimeter of a rectangular pool is 108 feet.
The length of the pool is 30 feet.

22. What is the width of the pool?

A. 24 ft.   C. 32 ft.

B. 26 ft.   D. 20 ft.

23. If the width and the length of the pool are 28 ft. and 32 ft. respectively, what is the perimeter of the pool?

A. 132 ft.   C. 94 ft.

B. 120 ft.   D. 60 ft.

24. What is the base of a triangle whose height is 15 inches and area is 60 square inches?

A. 4 in.   C. 8 in.

B. 12 in.   D. 9 in.

25. If the perimeter of a square is 36 feet, what is the area of the square?

A. 36 ft^2 C. 64 ft^2

B. 18 ft^2 D. 81 ft^2

26. Which of the following would be a non-standard unit of weight?

A. Gram   B. Fluid ounces

C. Liter

D. Brick

Tom sleeps for 8 hours and 15 minutes in a day.

27. How many hours did he sleep in four days?

A. 25.25 hours

C. 33 hours

B. 28.5 hours

D. 30.75 hours

28. How many hours did he sleep in one week?

A. 57.75 hours

C. 49.55 hours

B. 58.45 hours

D. 56.25 hours

29. How many seconds did he sleep in a day?

A. 28, 500 seconds

C. 28, 800 seconds

B. 29, 700 seconds

D. 28, 720 seconds

30. Mary has a fish tank with a capacity of 9 gallons. She uses a 4-cup bowl to fill the tank. How many bowls of water does she use?

A. 28

C. 38

B. 26

D. 36

The times in minutes it took for 8 participants to solve a puzzle are
10, 12, 13, 18, 9, 8, 9, and 9.

31. What is the mean of the data set?

A. 12.5

C. 11

B. 13

D. 10

32. What is the median of the data set?

A. 8.5

B. 10.5

C. 9.5   D. 9

33. What is the mode of the data set?

    A. 9   C. 10

    B. 8   D. There is no mode.

34. What is the range of the data set?

    A. 9   C. 8

    B. 10   D. 15

35. If the minimum value of the data set is removed, what is the mean of the data set?

    A. 12.5   C. 11

    B. 11.43   D. 12.16

36. If the minimum value of the data set is removed, what is the median of the data set?

    A. 9   C. 8

    B. 9.5   D. 10

Answer Key:

1. C	19. B
2. D	20. D
3. A	21. C
4. B	22. A
5. C	23. B
6. D	24. C
7. B	25. D
8. B	26. D
9. C	27. C
10. A	28. A
11. B	29. B
12. D	30. D
13. C	31. C
14. A	32. C
15. B	33. A
16. D	34. B
17. A	35. B
18. D	36. D

REFLECTION ON LEARNING

After completing Practice Test #2, reflect on your performance by answering the questions below. Discuss your responses with your instructor or a classmate.

1. What questions did you answer incorrectly? List the question numbers.

2. Review the list. What types of questions (operations, measurements, algebra, geometry, data analysis, statistics, graph, pie chart) did you answer incorrectly?

3. Review each question you've missed. Why do you think you answered the question incorrectly?

4. Based on the questions you missed, what math functions or concepts do you need to study and practice more? List them.

5. Review the question you got correctly. What strategies or methods did you use? What did you do well?

6. After reviewing all the questions, what questions do you have for your instructor?

You have 60 minutes to answer 36 questions.

1. What is another way to show or write 808, 560?

   A. 800,000 + 80,000 + 500 + 60

   B. 800,000 + 8,000 +500 + 60

   C. 88,000 + 5,000 + 600

   D. 800,000 + 800 + 600 + 60

2. In the number 56,748, what digit is in the tenth place?

   A. 4

   B. 5

   C. 6

   D. 8

3. What is the value of the underlined digit?

$$6,5\underline{3}8,112$$

   A. 3 thousand

   B. 30 hundred

   C. 30 thousand

   D. 300 thousand

4. There are 12, 566 foxes in a National Park. What is the correct way to write this number?

   A. Twelve thousand fifty hundred sixty-six

   B. Twelve hundred five thousand sixty-six

   C. Twelve thousand five hundred sixteen

   D. Twelve thousand five hundred sixty-six

5. Which of the following numbers is four hundred fifty-one thousand seventy-six?

   A. 451,760

   B. 451,076

   C. 415,076

   D. 451,067

6. Danielle bought a smart TV for $345 and sold it for $410. How much profit did she make?

   A. $105

   B. $60

   C. $45

   D. $65

7. Rick has 270 tickets for the summer fair, and each ride costs 6 tickets. How many rides can Rick go on?

   A. 45

   B. 55

   C. 42

   D. 48

8. Which of the following is a unit rate?

   A. 45 trucks per day

   B. 7/8

   C. 0.56

   D. 6 cups: 7 ounces

The cost of 65 raffle tickets was $780.

9. What is the cost of one ticket?

   A. $10

   B. $12

   C. $9

   D. $14

10. What is the cost of 20 tickets?

   A. $120

   B. $300

   C. $180

   D. $240

11. If Steve spends $156 on tickets, how many tickets did Steve buy?

   A. 13

   B. 8

   C. 15

   D. 7

Look at the following receipt:

```
                98788822
                HAPPY MART
                131 N MAIN ST
                SUMMERVILLE
ST#  1223  OP#  2112  TE#  1000  TR#

PRODUCT SERIAL # 1

PEANUTS                              2.46    T
PRODUCT SERIAL # 2

TOMATOES                             4.98    T
                        SUBTOTAL      ?
                  TAX   10.00 %      0.74
                           TOTAL     8.18
                      CASH TEND      0.00
                      DEBIT TEND     0.00
                     CHANGE DUE      0.00

EFT DEBIT          PAY FROM PRIMARY
0.00  TOTAL        PURCHASE
ACCOUNT #          131315
```

12. How many items were purchased?

    A. 3   C. 5

    B. 2   D. 4

13. What is the sub-total amount?

    A. $5.74   C. $6.44

    B. $8.66   D. $7.44

14. What is the total amount?

    A. $8.18   C. $6.44

    B. $7.76   D. $5.44

15. Which of the following is equal to 100 (30 − 17)?

    A. 100 (30) − 17   C. 130 − 1,700

    B. 3,000 − 1,700   D. 100 x 30 x 17

16. What is A + B?

$$2 \times 4 \times 6 \times 8 = A \times 2 \times 8 \times B$$

    A. 12   C. 16

    B. 24   D. 10

Look at the following modeling:

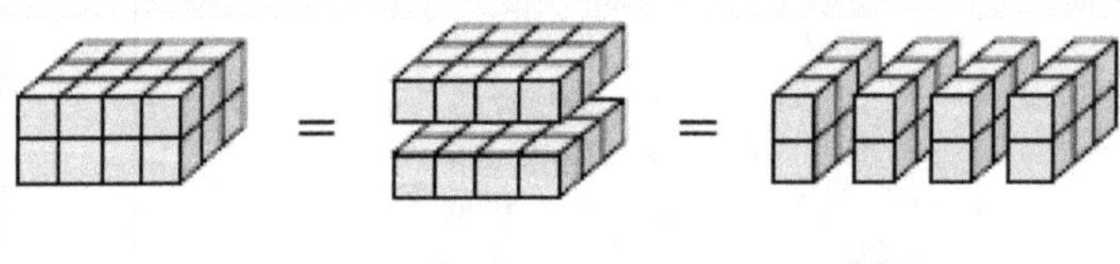

$$2 \cdot 3 \cdot 4 \quad = \quad 2 \cdot (3 \cdot 4) \quad = \quad ?$$

17. What is the missing expression?

    A. 4 + 3 + 2   C. 4 x (2 x 3)

    B. 3 x 4 x 2   D. 12

18. What property is shown?

    A. Commutative property of multiplication   C. Associative property of multiplication

    B. Commutative property of addition   D. Distributive property of multiplication

19. Solve the following equation:

$$12x + 80 = 224$$

A. x = 12   C. x = 16

B. x = 8   D. x = 7

20. Three times a number, decreased by 10, is equal to 53. What is the number?

A. 19   C. 24

B. 21   D. 17

In the following drawing, the distance between two horizontal dots or two vertical dots is 1 cm.

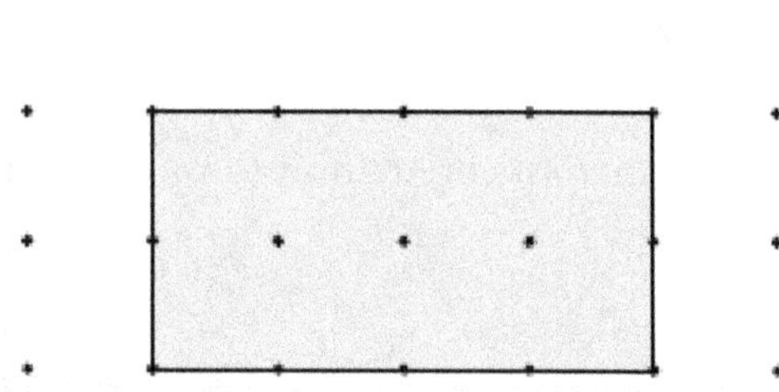

21. What is the perimeter of the rectangle?

A. 6 cm.   C. 15 cm.

B. 18 cm.   D. 12 cm.

22. What is the area of the rectangle?

A. 8 cm^2 C. 12 cm^2

B. 5 cm^2 D. 10 cm^2

23. What is the area of the following shape?

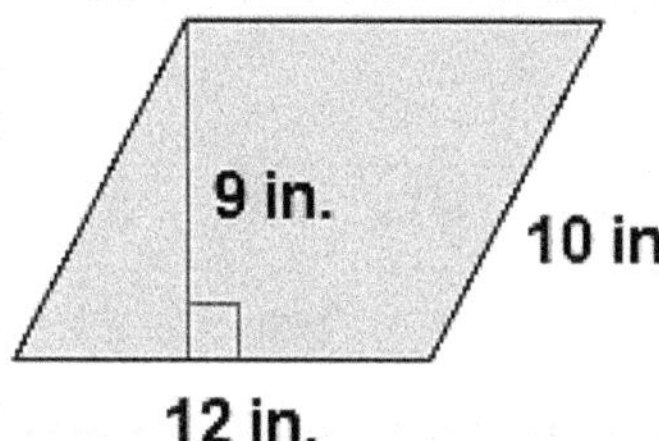

A. 120 in^2 C. 108 in^2

B. 54 in^2 D. 90 in^2

24. Which of the following is a metric unit of volume?

A. Cup

B. Barrel

C. Gram

D. Liter

25. Which of the following is true?

A. 10 gram = 1 kilogram

B. A liter is a metric unit of length.

C. 1,000 cm. = 1 m.

D. A hand span is a non-standard unit of length.

26. What is the missing value?

? Fluid ounces = 6 gallons

A. 768

B. 384

C. 72

D. 144

27. Which of the following would be an appropriate unit to measure the mass of an eraser?

A. Centimeter

B. Grams

C. Pounds

D. Kilograms

The following linear graph shows the amount of money donated to a charity:

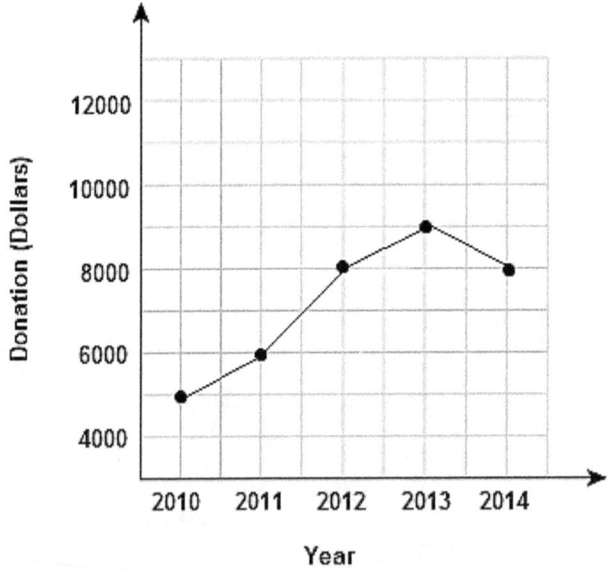

28. How much money was donated in 2011?

A. $5,000

B. $5,000

C. $6,000

D. $4,000

29. How much money was donated in 2013?

    A. $10,000   C. $8,000

    B. $9,500   D. $9,000

30. In what year did the charity receive $8,000?

    A. 2012   C. 2011

    B. 2014   D. 2010

31. In what year did the charity receive $5,000?

    A. 2014   C. 2010

    B. 2011   D. 2013

The following data set shows the test scores in a math class:

56, 77, 45, 87, 72, 90, 72, 66

32. What is the mean of the data set?

    A. 70   C. 71

    B. 72.50   D. 70.63

33. What is the median of the data set?

    A. 87   C. 72

    B. 45   D. 74

34. What is the mode of the data set?

    A. 72   C. 45

    B. 66   D. 56

35. What is the range of the data set?

    A. 90   C. 35

    B. 72   D. 45

36. If the minimum value of the data set is removed, what is the median of the data set?

    A. 66.5   C. 87

    B. 72   D. 66

Answer Key:

1. B	19. A
2. A	20. B
3. C	21. D
4. D	22. A
5. B	23. C
6. D	24. D
7. A	25. D
8. A	26. A
9. B	27. B
10. D	28. C
11. A	29. D
12. B	30. A
13. D	31. C
14. A	32. D
15. B	33. C
16. D	34. A
17. C	35. D
18. C	36. B

REFLECTION ON LEARNING

After completing Practice Test #3, reflect on your performance by answering the questions below. Discuss your responses with your instructor or a classmate.

1. What questions did you answer incorrectly? List the question numbers.

2. Review the list. What types of questions (operations, measurements, algebra, geometry, data analysis, statistics, graph, pie chart) did you answer incorrectly?

3. Review each question you've missed. Why do you think you answered the question incorrectly?

4. Based on the questions you missed, what math functions or concepts do you need to study and practice more? List them.

5. Review the question you got correctly. What strategies or methods did you use? What did you do well?

6. After reviewing all the questions, what questions do you have for your instructor?

You have 60 minutes to answer 36 questions.

1. What is another way to show or write $3,094,762$?

   A. $3,000,000 + 90,000 + 4,000 + 700 + 60 + 2$

   B. $3,000,000 + 900,000 + 4,000 + 700 + 60 + 2$

   C. $3,000,000 + 9,000 + 4,000 + 700 + 60 + 2$

   D. $300,000 + 900,000 + 4,000 + 700 + 60 + 2$

2. What is the missing value?

$$101,532 = ? + 1,000 + 500 + 30 + 2$$

   A. 10,000

   B. 110,000

   C. 1,000

   D. 100,000

3. What is the value of the underlined digit?

$$59,9\underline{2}7,168$$

   A. 2 thousand

   B. 20 hundred

   C. 20 thousand

   D. 200 thousand

4. Which number shows a 5 in the hundredths?

   A. 567

   B. 0.953

   C. 5,081

   D. 55,236

5. Which of the following numbers is one million five hundred sixty-seven thousand three hundred thirty-one?

   A. $1,576,331$

   B. $1,567,331$

   C. $1,657,331$

   D. $1,567,313$

6. Compute: $7 + 34 + 268$

   A. 309

   B. 299

   C. 318

   D. 329

7. A dog has a mass of 26 kilograms. The dog gains eight kilograms in one month and six kilograms the next month. What is the weight of the dog after the two months?

A. 38

B. 42

C. 40

D. 49

8. A software engineer installed 48 new systems three months ago and 134 new systems last month. How many more systems did the engineer install last month than three months ago?

A. 86

B. 182

C. 96

D. 79

9. A tank holds 2, 542 pounds of water. A cubic foot of water weighs 62 pounds. How many cubic feet of water does the tank hold?

A. 43 ft^3

B. 52 ft^3

C. 41 ft^3

D. 39 ft^3

10. It costs \$108 to buy 8 pizzas. What is the unit rate?

A. \$14 per pizza

B. \$13.50 per pizza

C. 3.5 pizzas per dollar

D. 13.5 pizzas per dollar

11. It rained 4.12 inches on Friday. On Saturday, it rained 1.46 inches less than on Friday. How much did it rain on Saturday?

A. 2.76 in.

B. 2.66 in.

C. 3.66 in.

D. 2.48 in.

12. Sean can run 6 miles in 0.75 hours. What is the unit rate in miles per hour?

A. 6.5 miles per hour

B. 4.5 miles per hour

C. 12 miles per hour

D. 8 miles per hour

13. Compute

$$\frac{3}{5} \times \left(\frac{1}{2} + \frac{3}{4} \right)$$

A. 3/4

B. 1/8

C. 5/4

D. 7/2

14. What is the missing value?

$$? \div \frac{1}{3} = \frac{2}{3}$$

A. 1/3

B. 1/6

C. 3/4

D. 2/9

15. Which of the following is equal to 45 + 99?

A. 5 (9 + 11)

B. 99 x 5

C. 9 (5 + 11)

D. 40 + 5 + (9 + 11)

16. What is the missing expression?

27 + (45 + 68) = ? + 45

A. 27 + 45

B. (27 + 68)

C. 27 x 68

D. 68 − 45

17. Which algebraic expression represents this phrase: "five times the sum of c and d"?

A. 5c + d

B. c + d + 5

C. c + 5d

D. 5 (c + d)

18. Which equation represents this phrase: "twice a number, increased by 34 is 87"?

A. 2x + 34 = 87

B. 2x - 34 = 87

C. x + 2 + 34 = 87

D. 34x + 2 = 87

19. Solve the following equation:

$$5x - 360 = 0$$

A. x = 86

B. x = 365

C. x = 72

D. x = 36

In the following drawing, the distance between two horizontal dots or two vertical dots is 1 cm.

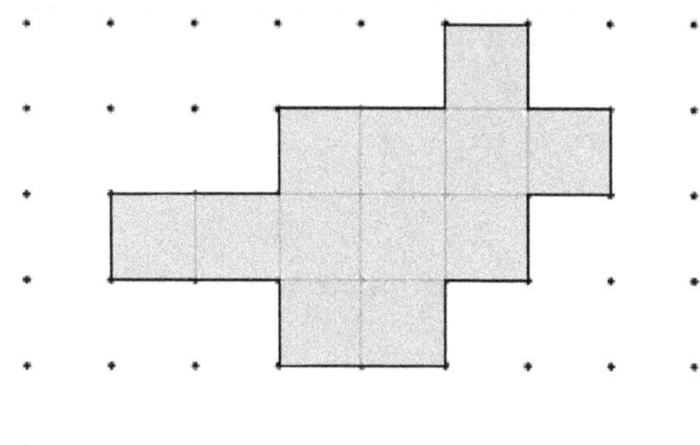

20. What is the perimeter of the shaded figure?

   A. 10 cm.

   B. 20 cm.

   C. 16 cm.

   D. 22 cm.

21. What is the area of the shaded figure?

   A. 8 cm^2

   B. 10 cm^2

   C. 13 cm^2

   D. 12 cm^2

22. What is the area of the following shape?

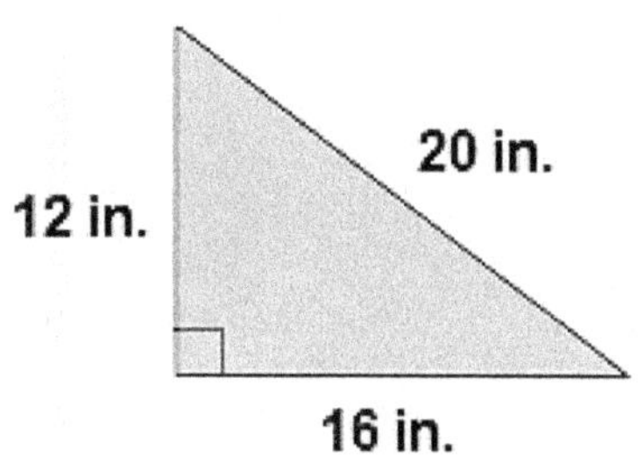

   A. 96 in^2

   B. 48 in^2

   C. 160 in^2

   D. 120 in^2

23. Which of the following is a metric unit of mass?

   A. Pound

   B. Kilogram

   C. Cubic feet

   D. Centimeter

24. Which of the following is true?

   A. 1 liter = 1 fluid ounces

   B. A yard is a metric unit of length.

   C. 1,000 m = 1 km

   D. A ruler is a non-standard unit of volume.

25. What is the missing value?

100 centimeters = ? millimeters

A. 1,000

B. 100

C. 10

D. 1

26. Which of the following would be an appropriate unit to measure the capacity of a contact lens case?

A. Quarts

B. Gallons

C. Pounds

D. Milliliters

27. Which of the following would be an appropriate unit to measure the capacity of a tanker truck?

A. Milligrams

B. Gallons

C. Cups

D. Feet

28. Charlie went to a party. It started at 8:30 p.m. and ended at 12:45 p.m. How long was the party?

A. 4 hours and 30 minutes

B. 4 hours and 45 minutes

C. 3 hours and 55 minutes

D. 4 hours and 15 minutes

29. How many minutes are there in a week?

A. 10, 080 minutes

B. 1, 440 minutes

C. 14, 400 minutes

D. 8, 640 minutes

30. The mean of the following data set is 45. What is the missing value?

23, 77, ?, 40, 30

A. 48

B. 45

C. 55

D. 68

31. The median of the following data set is 40. What is the missing value?

31, 70, 18, 20, ?, 68

A. 55

B. 91

C. 70

D. 49

The following data set represents the prices of gas in a city:

$3.45, $3.94, $3.12, $3.77, $4.05, $3.68, $3.35

32. What is the mean of the data set?

   A. $3.71

   B. $3.62

   C. $3.60

   D. $3.77

33. What is the median of the data set?

   A. $3.12

   B. $3.45

   C. $3.68

   D. $3.77

34. What is the mode of the data set?

   A. $3.94

   B. $3.45

   C. $4.05

   D. There is no mode.

35. What is the range of the data set?

   A. $4.05

   B. $0.93

   C. $1.18

   D. $3.12

36. If the maximum value of the data set is removed, what is the median of the data set?

   A. $3.55

   B. $3.57

   C. $3.62

   D. $3.68

Answer Key:

1. A	19. C
2. D	20. B
3. C	21. D
4. B	22. A
5. B	23. B
6. A	24. C
7. C	25. A
8. A	26. D
9. C	27. B
10. B	28. D
11. B	29. A
12. D	30. C
13. A	31. D
14. D	32. B
15. C	33. C
16. B	34. D
17. D	35. B
18. A	36. B

REFLECTION ON LEARNING

After completing Practice Test #4, reflect on your performance by answering the questions below. Discuss your responses with your instructor or a classmate.

1. What questions did you answer incorrectly? List the question numbers.

2. Review the list. What types of questions (operations, measurements, algebra, geometry, data analysis, statistics, graph, pie chart) did you answer incorrectly?

3. Review each question you've missed. Why do you think you answered the question incorrectly?

4. Based on the questions you missed, what math functions or concepts do you need to study and practice more? List them.

5. Review the question you got correctly. What strategies or methods did you use? What did you do well?

6. After reviewing all the questions, what questions do you have for your instructor?

ADULT ED
MATH
NUMBER SYSTEM, NUMBER SENSE,
AND OPERATIONS PREPARING
FOR
CASAS, TABE 11 & 12,
HISET, AND GED TESTING
BY COACHING FOR BETTER LEARNING

ADULT ED
MATH
GEOMETRY PREPARING
FOR
CASAS, TABE 11 & 12,
HISET, AND GED TESTING
BY COACHING FOR BETTER LEARNING

CBL COACHING
Math
Practice Worksheets and
Workbook for Adult
Students

SKILLS FOR SUCCESS
IN CAREER AND
TECHNICAL EDUCATION (CTE)
STUDENT
GUIDE
A SYSTEMATIC
WAY TO MASTER
ORGANIZATIONAL AND SOFT SKILLS
CBL COACHING

HOW TO
ACHIEVE
BETTER
STUDENT
RETENTION
IN ADULT
EDUCATION
Secrets to becoming
an indispensable
adult-ed teacher that
provides a learning
experience that's hard
to walk away from (and
keeps administrators
happy!)
TEDDY EDOUARD

TABE 11 & 12
CONSUMABLE
STUDENT READING
MANUAL
FOR LEVEL E
By Coaching for Better Learning, LLC

TABE 11 & 12
CONSUMABLE
STUDENT READING
MANUAL
FOR LEVEL M
By Coaching for Better Learning, LLC

TABE 11 & 12
CONSUMABLE
STUDENT READING
MANUAL
FOR LEVEL D
By Coaching for Better Learning, LLC

TABE 11 & 12
STUDENT
LANGUAGE
MANUAL
FOR LEVEL E
By Coaching for Better Learning, LLC

TABE 11 & 12
STUDENT
LANGUAGE
MANUAL
FOR LEVEL M
By Coaching for Better Learning, LLC

TABE 11 & 12 Math Tests
TABE 11 & 12
Consumable
Student Math
Workbook
FOR LEVEL E
By Coaching
for Better Learning, LLC

TABE 11 & 12 Math Tests
TABE 11 & 12
Consumable
Student Math
Workbook
FOR LEVEL M
By Coaching
for Better Learning, LLC

TABE 11 & 12 Math Tests
TABE 11 & 12
Consumable
Student Math
Workbook
FOR LEVEL D
By Coaching
for Better Learning, LLC

PRACTICE TESTS FOR
CASAS MATH GOAL 2
Level A–Forms 921M and 922M
CBL COACHING

CBL COACHING
Workbook
Number and Letter Tracing
for
Adult Students

READING
NOTEBOOK
&
JOURNAL
For Adult Students
By Coaching For Better Learning CBL COACHING

MATH NOTEBOOK
& JOURNAL
For Adult Students
By Coaching For Better Learning CBL COACHING

BOOK 1
PHONICS AND LIFE SKILLS READING
FOR
Adult Literacy, ABE, and ESL Students
Turning Learners into Proficient Readers
CBL COACHING

BOOK 2
PHONICS AND LIFE SKILLS READING
FOR
Adult Literacy, ABE, and ESL Students
Turning Learners into Proficient Readers
CBL COACHING

BOOK 3
PHONICS AND LIFE SKILLS READING
FOR
Adult Literacy, ABE, and ESL Students
Turning Learners into Proficient Readers
CBL COACHING

CBL equips programs and instructors to increase student retention, learning—and success.

We do it by offering evidence-based systematic solutions, learner-centered teaching materials, instructor-centered training, and future-oriented strategies in adult education, workforce development, and vocational training.

We teach proven insights, knowledge, and skills that are useful to practitioners (instructors, administrators, and support staff).

CBL also takes pride in publishing student-centered textbooks designed to prepare learners for CASAS, TABE 11&12, HiSET, and GED assessments and assist instructors in covering course curricula and standards with confidence.

Our publications also include teaching guides, test prep tools, and study guides that foster reflective learning, ensuring sustained engagement in active learning. Find our meticulously crafted textbooks on our book page (cbledu.com) or major platforms like Amazon, Barnes & Noble, and Ingram Spark.

CBL also guides adult education and workforce programs in establishing robust professional development programs—training, peer-mentoring, coaching, community of practices (CoPs), and instructional systems— fostering a culture of continuous improvement and contributing to higher learner retention and success rates. We also offer workshops and PD sessions for adult educators and classroom instructors.

If you have suggestions or questions about instructional systems, textbooks, or student learning and retention, contact us today at teamcbl@cbledu.com or 410-960-4082.